GLOBAL ISSUES

Series editors: Stephen Ha

ENVIRONMENTAL STEWARDSHIP

Ruth Goring Stewart

6 Studies
for individuals
or groups

INTERVARSITY PRESS
DOWNERS GROVE, ILLINOIS 60515

InterVarsity Press is the book-publishing division of InterVarsity Christian Fellowship, a student movement active on campus at hundreds of universities, colleges and schools of nursing in the United States of America, and a member movement of the International Fellowship of Evangelical Students. For information about local and regional activities, write Public Relations Dept., InterVarsity Christian Fellowship, 6400 Schroeder Rd., P.O. Box 7895, Madison, WI 53707-7895.

All Scripture quotations, unless otherwise indicated, are from the Holy Bible, New International Version. Copyright © 1973, 1978, International Bible Society. Used by permission of Zondervan Bible Publishers.

Cover illustration: TransLight

ISBN 0-8308-4903-3

Printed in the United States of America

12	11	10	9	8	7	6	5	4	3	2	1
99	98	97	96	95	94	93	92	91	90		

Contents

Because humankind is made in the image of God, every person, regardless of race, religion, color, culture, class, sex or age, has an intrinsic dignity because of which he or she should be respected and served, not exploited. Here too we express penitence both for our neglect and for having sometimes regarded evangelism and social concern as mutually exclusive.

Although reconciliation with people is not reconciliation with God, nor is social action evangelism, nor is political liberation salvation, nevertheless we affirm that evangelism and sociopolitical involvement are both part of our Christian duty. For both are necessary expressions of our doctrines of God and humankind, our love for our neighbor and our obedience to Jesus Christ.

The message of salvation implies also a message of judgment upon every form of alienation, oppression and discrimination, and we should not be afraid to denounce evil and injustice wherever they exist.

—*Lausanne Covenant, Article Five.*

Welcome to Global Issues Bible Studies

With all the rapid and dramatic changes happening in our world today, it's easy to be overwhelmed and simply withdraw. But it need not be so for Christians! God has not only given us the mandate to love the world, he has given us the Holy Spirit and the community of fellowship to guide us and equip us in the ministry of love.

Ministering in the world can be threatening: It requires change in both our lifestyle and our thinking. We end up discovering that we need to cling closer to Jesus than ever before—and that becomes the great personal benefit of change. God's love for the world is the same deep love he has for you and me.

This study series is designed to help us understand what is going on in *the world*. Then it takes us to *the Word* to help us be faithful in our compassionate response. The series is firmly rooted in the evangelical tradition which calls for a personal saving relationship with Jesus Christ and a public lifestyle of discipleship that demonstrates the Word has truly come alive in us.

At the front of the guide is an excerpt from the Lausanne Covenant which we have found helpful. We have developed this series in keeping with the spirit of the covenant, especially sections four and five. You may wish to refer to the Lausanne Covenant for further guidance as you form your own theology of evangelism and social concern.

In the words of the covenant's authors we challenge you: "The salvation we claim should be transforming us in the totality of our personal and social responsibilities. Faith without works is dead."

Getting the Most from Global Issues Bible Studies

Global Issues Bible Studies are designed to be an exciting and challenging way to help us seek God's will for all of the world as it is found in Scripture. As we learn more about the world, we will learn more about ourselves as well.

How They Are Designed

Global Issues Bible Studies have a number of distinctive features. First, each guide has an introduction from the author which will help orient us to the significant questions which the studies will deal with.

Second, the Bible study portion is inductive rather than deductive. The author will lead us to discover what the Bible says about a particular topic through a series of questions rather than simply telling us what he or she believes. Therefore, the studies are thought-provoking. They help us to think about the meaning of the passage so that we can truly understand what the biblical writer intended to say.

Third, the studies are personal. Global Issues Bible Studies are not just theoretical studies to be considered in private or discussed in a group. These studies will motivate us to action. They will expose us to the promises, assurances, exhortations and challenges of God's Word. Through the study of Scripture, we will renew our minds so that we can be transformed by the Spirit of God.

Fourth, the guides include resource sections that will help you to act on the challenges Scripture has presented you with.

Fifth, these studies are versatile. They are designed for student, mission, neighborhood and/or church groups. They are also effective for individual study.

How They Are Put Together

Global Issues Bible Studies also have a distinctive format. Each study need take no more than forty-five minutes in a group setting or thirty minutes in personal study—unless you choose to take more time.

Each guide has six studies. If the guides are used in pairs, they can be used within a quarter system in a church and fit well in a semester or trimester system on a college campus.

The guides have a workbook format with space for writing responses. This is ideal for personal study and lets group members prepare in advance for the discussion. In addition the last question in each study offers suggestions and opportunity for personal response.

At the end of the guides are some notes for leaders. They describe how to lead a group discussion, give helpful tips on group dynamics and suggest ways to deal with problems which may arise during the discussion. With such helps, someone with little or no experience can lead an effective study.

Suggestions for Individual Study

1. As you begin, pray that God will help you understand and apply the passages to your life. Pray that he will show you what kinds of action he would have you take as a result of your time of study.

2. In your first session take time to read the introduction to the entire guide. This will orient you to the subject at hand and the author's goals for the studies.

3. Read the short introduction to the study.

4. Read and reread the suggested Bible passages to familiarize yourself with them.

5. A good modern translation of the Bible, rather than the King James Version or a paraphrase, will give you the most help. The New International Version, the New American Standard Bible and the Revised Standard Version are all recommended. The questions in this guide are based on the New International Version.

6. Use the space provided to respond to the questions. This will help you express your understanding of the passage clearly.

7. Look up the passages listed under *For Further Study* at the end of each study. This will help you to better understand the principles outlined in the main passages and give you an idea of how these

themes are found throughout Scripture.

8. It might be good to have a Bible dictionary handy. Use it to look up any unfamiliar words, names or places.

9. Take time with the final question in each study to commit yourself to action and/or a change in attitude.

Suggestions for Group Study

1. Come to the study prepared. Follow the suggestions for individual study mentioned above. You will find that careful preparation will greatly enrich your time spent in group discussion.

2. Be willing to participate in the discussion. The leader of your group will not be lecturing. Instead, he or she will be encouraging the members of the group to discuss what they have learned. The leader will be asking the questions that are found in this guide.

3. Stick to the topic being discussed. Your answers should be based on the verses which are the focus of the discussion and not on outside authorities such as commentaries or speakers.

4. Be sensitive to the other members of the group. Listen attentively when they describe what they have learned. You may be surprised by their insights! When possible, link what you say to the comments of others. Also, be affirming whenever you can. This will encourage some of the more hesitant members of the group to participate.

5. Be careful not to dominate the discussion. We are sometimes so eager to express our thoughts that we leave too little opportunity for others to respond. By all means participate! But allow others to also.

6. Expect God to teach you through the passage being discussed and through the group. Pray that you will have an enjoyable and profitable time together, but also that as a result of the study, you will find ways that you can take action individually and/or as a group.

7. If you are the discussion leader, you will find additional suggestions at the back of the guide.

God bless you in your adventure of love.

Steve Hayner and Gordon Aeschliman

Introducing Environmental Stewardship

The care of the earth is our most ancient and most worthy and, after all, our most pleasing responsibility. To cherish what remains of it, and to foster its renewal, is our only legitimate hope.

—Wendell Berry

This week's newspapers for my city in the Los Angeles area report that an oil tanker spilled thousands of barrels of crude oil in Newport Harbor. The slick has fragmented; parts of it are coming dangerously close to a wildlife refuge that is a haven for several endangered species. Meanwhile, ad hoc neighborhood groups are gathering to protest the spraying of the pesticide malathion over residential areas— a state-mandated measure to attempt to eradicate the Mediterranean fruit fly, a threat to citrus crops. Protesters are claiming that they have suffered headaches, nausea and other ill-effects from their exposure to the poison. These effects on humans are disputed, but it is known that malathion kills ladybugs and other beneficial insects.

Additionally, every day the city of Los Angeles releases eight hundred million gallons of treated sewage into Santa Monica Bay. Accidental releases of raw sewage are not uncommon. The whole world's oceans—and the species they contain—are at risk because of such human activity. For instance, techniques for catching tuna cause the deaths of thousands of dolphins every year. Overfishing has in many parts of the world reduced fish populations so much that local economies are severely affected: in Namibia, for example, the fishing industry's contribution to the gross domestic product fell from twenty per cent in the 1970s to only five per cent in the 1980s.

Fresh water is equally endangered. Only about one per cent of the world's water is drinkable, and pollution affects a significant proportion of that. Bacterial and viral contamination of water is a major cause of death throughout much of the Third World. Recent government studies in southern California's San Gabriel Valley have concluded that it will be impossible to remove chemical pollution from area wells. The subsurface sand and gravel are porous, so that the noxious chemicals have spread freely, permeating the aquifer.

Another aspect of the crisis is that we have simply been using too much water. The water table in the American Great Plains is being drastically depleted by irrigation. In some areas of western Kansas the Ogallala Aquifer, a layer of sand and gravel that serves as the groundwater source for farmlands from North Dakota to Texas, has dropped as much as two hundred feet—a fifty per cent loss of saturation—since the 1940s when widespread irrigation began.

Analysts acknowledge that the farm economy has become much too reliant on crops that are actually not suitable to the Great Plains' essentially arid climate. Meanwhile, irrigation is causing salinization of the soil rendering it less and less fit for bearing any crops at all. Heavy use of pesticides and herbicides has had negative effects upon the balance of nature—the delicate equilibrium among populations of insects, animals and plants. Serious questions have also been raised about these substances' effects on human health.

Further, our cities' landfills are bursting. Because they are being filled so rapidly, even biodegradable garbage is being insulated from the sun and the rain that would aid the process of degradation. Toxic chemicals and bacteria seep into the groundwater under these dumps.

Amazonian rain forests are being destroyed at a rapid rate in order to harvest exotic woods and provide grazelands for cattle. (Some of these cattle eventually end up as beef for North American fast-food). It is estimated that this deforestation causes the extinction of three tropical species every day. Plants incorporate carbon dioxide and produce oxygen; the wide-scale burning of forests, then, leads to an imbalance in the earth's atmosphere. The resulting "greenhouse effect" is still being debated by scientists; it has been suggested, for example, that global warming will change climate patterns and lead to the melting of ice caps and a corresponding rise in sea levels.

Then there is acid rain, the depletion of ozone, soil erosion, nuclear waste, the shipping of chemical wastes to the Third World, and the explosion of new biotechnologies whose environmental effects are not yet known. The problems are enormous. What caused this crisis? What attitudes and values have led to the poisoning of our planet? And, beyond the desire to survive, does the Bible offer Christians any compelling teachings that might guide and motivate us to begin caring more responsibly for the earth?

A Legacy of Exploitation

Some have laid blame for the environmental disaster at the door of the church. In an influential essay Lynn White, Jr., charged that the Bible teaches that human beings are to take dominion over nature and exploit it. This doctrine, he said, undergirds practices such as strip-mining, chemical dumping and overfarming. If one were in search of a spiritual foundation for a more responsible approach to earthkeeping, then, the Bible would not be the place to look.[1]

Poet-farmer Wendell Berry rejects that interpretation. He sees our violence against nature as rooted not in biblical teaching but in the patterns of colonialism the Europeans brought with them to the New World. White Americans ever since, he says, have been preoccupied with conquering, exploiting and moving on. The Industrial Revolution and the development of free-market capitalism played into the pattern: short-term profits became all-important, and work became more specialized and increasingly divorced from the land. Thus land became merely something to be used; fewer and fewer individuals had a direct relationship with it. We surrendered our birthright—our intimate relationship with the earth—and allowed the land to be stripped, poisoned and abused. What's more, we exported our irresponsible practices, and now the crisis is worldwide in scope.

The church is certainly not blameless. Some Christians have indeed used the words *have dominion* and *subdue* from the King James Version of Genesis to justify exploitive practices. Even when secular movements arose to call Western society to a new sense of environmental responsibility, the church was all too slow to respond.

The ecology movement of the early 1970s was castigated by many for its faddishness and romanticism. Certainly many of its proponents failed to think through the implications of their newfound values. I remember a non-Christian friend of mine, pregnant and under pressure from her activist boyfriend to have an abortion, commenting ruefully that he had more compassion for baby seals than for baby human beings.

Such inconsistencies were seized upon by many Christians as an excuse for ignoring the ecological crisis. In reality, however, few of us were willing to commit ourselves to a re-evaluation of our theology of creation, our country's public policies regarding the environment, or our own wasteful lifestyles. Many of us thought Jesus' return was imminent. If we could expect him any day, wasn't saving souls more important than saving an earth that would soon be burned up anyway?

Questions like these are still being asked in Christian circles. Such questions betray a profound, often unconscious, theological misunderstanding of the nature of physical reality and indeed the scope of Jesus' work of redemption.

The speculations of classical Greek philosophers influenced the thinking of many of the church fathers and remain embedded in many Christians' world views today. Plato's teachings suggested the inferiority of matter and thus of the body. Only the spirit of man was immortal, capable of reaching toward the Ideal. (I use the masculine form here as Plato did; he had a low view of women.) Some of the New Testament Epistles were written specifically to counter neo-Platonic teachings such as those of the Gnostics, who because of their belief that matter is illusory, denied the Incarnation. It seemed impossible and even indecent that a God who was perfect Spirit should soil himself by taking on human flesh.

The Scriptures do insist that physical reality is not all of reality and that the creation must never become an idol. In explaining humankind's rebellion against God, the apostle Paul deplores the fact that men and women "exchanged the truth of God for a lie, and worshiped and served created things rather than the Creator" (Rom 1:25). "For what is seen is temporary," Paul asserts in 2 Corinthians 4:18, "but what is unseen is eternal." Creation is finite. Only the Creator is perfect; only he is the source of our salvation.

If we are not to be Gnostics, yet we are also not to elevate the creation as an object of worship, how then are we to treat nature? The Bible studies that follow will suggest several answers to this question: We are to *use* the creation. We are to *serve* and *tend* it. We are to *celebrate* it. And we are to *listen* to it.

Learning to See

A new humility is crucial as we begin to learn our responsibilities toward the earth. We have failed badly. We have allowed the earth, our God-given home, to be ravaged. We have ignored biblical teaching and have mindlessly joined in the pursuit of the American dream with all its material wastefulness and spiritual impoverishment. Like the church in Laodicea, we have come to think complacently, "I am rich. I have acquired wealth and do not need a thing." The prophetic message warns, "But you do not realize that you are wretched, pitiful, poor, blind and naked" (Rev 3:17).

We are blind . . . and the process of learning to see, and to act on our new insight, will be difficult and sometimes painful. We will have to submit to Jesus Christ our attitudes toward his creation, allowing him to lead our thoughts captive (2 Cor 10:5). We need to work our way toward a fully biblical theology of creation. This task is not just for seminary professors but indeed for every Christian. I am not reading my Bible properly if I skip over what it tells me about the interrelationships among God, humankind and the physical world.

Thinking and doing in Scripture are integrally connected. "Anyone who listens to the word but does not do what it says is like a man who looks at his face in a mirror and, after looking at himself, goes away and immediately forgets what he looks like" (Jas 1:23-24). A new theology must become a new way of living.

Learning to Love

The prospect is daunting. That spill in Newport Harbor poured nearly 400,000 gallons of oil onto the ocean's surface. Rain-forest species are being depleted at the rate of more than one thousand per year. The so-called Superfund is minuscule in relation to the vast need for cleanup of toxic wastes in American cities. And I am only one person. My small group is only eight people. Where do we start?

Better to ask, *how* do we start? We start with love: love for the world that God loves. The interesting thing about love is that *it always fastens upon the particular*. General feelings of benevolence and goodwill that have no concrete expression in relation to a specific loved object are mere sentimentality. This truth is well put in the tongue-in-cheek words of a common saying: "I love mankind. It's my next-door neighbor I can't stand."

God loves us concretely. "God so loved the world," says John 3:16—a sweeping statement. This magnificent, extravagant love was expressed, however, in an act that was concrete and limited: he sent his Son to a particular family at a particular time in history, to live in a particular place—Nazareth, a cultural and political backwater. Jesus, the carrier of the Father's all-embracing love, never traveled far. He spent most of his time with twelve men, and perhaps an equal number of women were devoted to him.

Even an infinite God loves the specific, the particular, the concrete. Surely then we can accept our limitations and commit our love to a few particular needs, through a few concrete actions.

Personal Lifestyle, Public Policy

If the devastation of creation is to be reversed or even mitigated, changes will be required at the individual, community, national and international levels.

On a personal level, each of us must pursue simplicity of life. Writers such as Ron Sider, Tom Sine and Richard Foster have for some time been calling us to reduce our consumption, both for our own spiritual health and to promote economic justice. There is a further motivation: our excessive consumption has been poisoning the earth.

A college professor was once asked what kind of lifestyle would promote environmental responsibility. He summed it up in two words: "convivial austerity." I like this phrase because it is reminiscent of much that Jesus taught. Biblical simplicity requires abandoning possessions for the sake of the kingdom. But our simplicity is indeed to be convivial: sharing what we have, developing solidarity with the poor, and celebrating our community and need for one another.

But small-scale acts are not enough. Christians who care about the earth must examine laws and practices in the wider community and call for changes. The U.S. government, as with others, has been quite recalcitrant in the matter of negotiating international agreements to reduce acid rain, ban chemical dumping and stop the development of biological and chemical weapons. Congress and the executive branch have been slow in approving legislation to clean our air. But lawmakers are responsive to pressure; we must learn to use our power as constituents. There is strength, too, in unity: established groups like Sierra Club are experienced in lobbying. Smaller ad hoc groups are good places to form relationships while addressing local needs.

The response questions at the end of each Bible study will help you get a start in this process. They suggest many specific ways in which we can learn to love the earth, both personally and corporately.

A Call to Joy

It is easy to grow discouraged. Love of the earth calls for sacrifice—giving up some of our time, energy and possessions in order to live in a responsible relationship with the rest of creation. Sometimes our efforts seem futile. Much as we try to focus on loving the particular and accepting our limitations, we're still aware that smog continues to blanket our cities, toxic chemicals continue to be dumped in the Third World, and the pollution of our valleys' wells is so pervasive that it cannot be addressed by existing technology.

How can our hope be renewed?

We must develop *listening hearts* to hear God's promises in the biblical revelation and the daily revelation of his faithfulness through his handiwork—his creation, the very object of our newfound concern and love.

God made the earth, and he has not abandoned it. To the cowering Job he thunders:

Who cuts a channel for the torrents of rain,
    and a path for the thunderstorm,
to water a land where no man lives,
    a desert with no one in it,
to satisfy a desolate wasteland
    and make it sprout with grass?

    Does the rain have a father?
Who fathers the drops of dew?
From whose womb comes the ice?

Who gives birth to the frost from the heavens
    when the waters become hard as stone,
when the surface of the deep is frozen? (Job 38:25-30)

The questions are merely rhetorical. Their answer is clear. *It is God who fathers and mothers the earth.* He is continually giving birth to it, continually fashioning and nurturing it. Our work in attempting to undo the devastation of sin in our world is only a part of a great work that has been ongoing since the first day of creation.

We serve a great God, a God of boundless creative energy. We have not been left to our own resources. Nature serves us by reminding us of these truths, refreshing our bodies and spirits, calling us into joy.

Learning to heed that call—to take time to garden, to hike, to listen to the rain, to wade along a rocky beach—is not mere sentimentality or frivolous self-indulgence. The writers of the psalms were exquisitely attuned to God's voice in nature and nature's joyful response:

Let the sea resound, and everything in it,
   the world, and all who live in it.
Let the rivers clap their hands,
   let the mountains sing together for joy;
let them sing before the LORD,
   for he comes to judge the earth.
He will judge the world in righteousness
   and the peoples with equity. (Ps 98:7-9)

"For all this," wrote poet Gerard Manley Hopkins—all this industrial waste, this pollution, this chasm that has developed between humankind and the rest of creation—"nature is never spent; / There lives the dearest freshness deep down things." That freshness is a gift to us, a source of renewal. We can experience it by hiking through the Rockies, but it is also present in the intricate pattern of veins on the leaf of a houseplant. In spite of our sin, in spite of our abuse of God's world, that promise of new life is all around us.

"God is king," sing the snowflakes, the roadside weeds, the mountains. "He mothers us, fathers us. He has not left us; his kingdom is here, is coming. He gives life. He renews the world. Praise him, and take heart! Alleluia, alleluia."

---

[1]Lynn White, Jr., "The Historical Roots of Our Ecological Crisis," in *Science,* 1967.

Study 1
The Artist's Hand

Christians *have focused much attention on the first few chapters of* Genesis in the debate between creationism and evolution. In focusing on this aspect of Genesis, however, we overlook the aspects of God's character which are revealed in these chapters. Genesis 1 and 2 paint a picture of an exuberant artist, alternately shaping and standing back to admire his great work. More than God's *method,* these chapters describe God's attitude toward his creation.

Read Genesis 1:1—2:25.
1. What evidence do you find in Genesis 1 for the nature and participation of the Godhead in creation?

2. Genesis 1 is a very rhythmic, repetitious passage. What are the key words and phrases that recur throughout this chapter?

3. How does God respond to the world and its creatures as he brings them forth? (Refer to your list of key phrases; also see 1:22.)

4. What part does language play in the creative process chronicled here (1:5, 8)?

5. In what way does God allow Adam to share in the creative process (2:19-20)?

How is this task ongoing for human beings?

6. How does God bring animals, plants and human beings deeper into relationship with one another (1:29-30)?

7. The Hebrew word translated "rule" in 1:26 suggests the responsibilities of a king. God, the Great King, has given humankind a kingly position within creation. If we were to begin to fulfill that responsibility by modeling ourselves on God's own attitudes and actions in this passage, how might our kingship be expressed?

8. In 2:15, the word translated "to work," *abad,* means "to serve" and is related to a noun that means "slave" or "servant." What light does this shed on our kingly responsibilities to the earth?

9. Make a list of this passage's teachings regarding the relationship between human beings and the rest of the created order.

In what ways do we fail to uphold our end of this relationship?

10. *Response:* Take a hike in the hills or just a stroll through a city park. Sit down on the grass or on a rock and contemplate your surroundings—the variegations in a rock, the patterns of tree bark, the veins of a leaf. Think of the pleasure God took in creating these things.

For Further Study: John 1:1-3.

Study 2

The Dance of Creation

Healthy Christians meditate on and speak often of God's love for human beings. We are all wounded and needy, and the miracle of our Father's tenderness toward us is the beginning and end of our healing. When we know—really know—that we are loved deeply and passionately, we are empowered to begin loving and serving others.

Yet most of us have not realized how wildly extravagant God's love is. He is in relationship not only with us, but also with the whole of creation.

We in the West tend to think of nature as essentially inanimate. Scripture, however, offers a different picture. We need to expand our concept of "we" and "us"—to see humans as fellow creatures with the rest of creation, partners in a great dance of love, praise, service, sacrifice and gratitude, mirroring the delight the Father, Son and Holy Spirit have taken in one another for all eternity.

Read Psalm 104.

1. Make a list of the verbs describing God's activity in nature (vv. 2-14, 27-32).

2. During the eighteenth century, in Europe and North America the idea became current that God was a Great Watchmaker—having created an intricately designed earth, he wound it up and essentially left it to run itself. Based on your list from question 1, replace the title "Great Watchmaker" with titles that more biblically reflect God's ongoing relationship with his creation.

3. List the phrases in Psalm 104 that have to do with nature's response to God's care (vv. 7-15, 27-32).

4. How would you describe nature's relationship to God?

5. How does God draw nature into his service (vv. 2-4)?

6. How might our actions toward the earth change if we were to treat it, for example, as God's garment (v. 2)?

7. Identify the verses that bring humans into the dance—showing our relationship to nature and to nature's Creator (see, for example, verse 14).

8. Do you think the "they" which is referred to in verses 27-30 includes humanity as well as nature? Why?

9. Whether you are alone or in a group, read aloud Psalm 96 and spend time worshiping God for his generous sustenance of his creatures.

10. *Response:* Choose one or more of the following activities as a group or on your own.

☐ Do a little housecleaning of God's tent. Take a walk and pick up litter as you go or find a vacant lot that needs some cleanup and go to it.

☐ Contact a local biologist or conservation group and find out whether any plant or animal species in your area is endangered because of human activity, and what you can do about it.

☐ Keep track of your car's mileage and have it checked for polluting emissions. Can you use less gas by taking the bus, riding a bike or walking?

For Further Study: Job 38—41.

Study 3

A Garden to Tend

For many of us, farming—even gardening—is an alien occupation practiced by loners who wear flannel shirts and overalls and are separated from neighbors by many miles. Industrialized countries are by definition more industrial than agricultural. Few citizens of industrialized nations are involved in the work of caring for the land and reaping its fruits. Their numbers continue to diminish as large corporations, relying on complex machinery and (in some areas) the help of a migrant underclass, take over the job of producing food.

Many have hailed these developments as progress—"liberating" the majority of the population from hard physical labor. Yet more and more we are recognizing that it is not so simple. Changes in farming practices have affected us all. We eat foods that carry residues of herbicides and pesticides—the long-term effects of which are not known. Tropical rain forests are destroyed to provide us with cheap hamburgers; climates a continent away are affected, and the earth's ability to cycle and clean our air is weakened.

And most of us live severed from the earth, unaware of our profound daily dependence on its bounty.

God gave Israel, an agricultural society, guidelines for establishing just and healthy farming practices. Perhaps, after all, even those of us who are urban need to understand what constitutes wholesome agriculture.

Read Leviticus 25:1-7.
1. What is the primary way the Israelites are to care for their land (vv. 3-4, 11)?

2. What would a sabbath year for the land be like for the people of Israel (vv. 4-7)?

Read Leviticus 25:8-24.
3. What are the key provisions of the Year of Jubilee (vv. 13-22)?

4. How do the guidelines for observing the Year of Jubilee show the link that exists between care of the land and justice for people?

5. In what ways can you see that link continuing to exist today?

How is the misuse of land related to the oppression of people?

6. Why does God say that he is establishing these rules regarding the land (v. 23)?

7. What images does the phrase "redemption of the land" bring to mind (v. 24)?

8. How might modern farms look different if our society were to begin applying some of the principles of Leviticus 25?

How might your life be different?

9. *Response:* Choose one or more of the following activities to do as a group or on your own.

☐ Talk to your grocer. Explain to him or her that you want organically grown produce and that you are willing to pay more for the smaller-scale methods of production that requires.

☐ Do a bit of your own gardening. Plant a corner of your yard or borrow a corner of someone else's. Learn what crops thrive in your climate, what pests might be likely to attack them, and how you might combat those pests with little or no resort to chemicals. Find out what organic fertilizers are readily accessible.

☐ If you prepare your own food, begin composting vegetable wastes (such as rinds, pulp, eggshells and seeds). This need not be an overwhelmingly complex process. Simply bury your wastes in your gardening area, or deliver them regularly to a friend who gardens.

☐ Talk to a Christian farmer about the issues he or she faces in working the land lovingly.

The Land
in Mourning

Given the interconnectedness we have begun to see among God, human beings and nature, it comes as no surprise that the sin of humanity has affected not only our relationships with God and each other, but also our relationship to the rest of creation.

C. S. Lewis pictures it well in The Chronicles of Narnia. In *The Lion, the Witch and the Wardrobe* we see that under the dominion of the White Witch, the land falls into a perpetual silent winter. In *The Last Battle* when the false Aslan gains power, one of the first signs of evil is that the Talking Trees begin to be felled.

We cannot contain our sin. It blights everything we touch.

Read Isaiah 5:7-16.

1. Verse 7 gives a general context for the woes that follow. In verse

8, how are the recipients of the Lord's judgment described?

2. What is their principal sin and against whom and what is it being committed? (For a reminder of the laws that these people are violating, review Leviticus 25 in study three.)

3. Summarize the two judgments that the Lord pronounces on those who "add house to house" and "join field to field" (vv. 9-10).

4. What contemporary practices are analogous to the sin described in verse 8? (Consider the acquisitive materialism of Western lifestyles, and think about agricultural businesses and how our food is produced.)

How do our consumption and lifestyle patterns implicate us in the destructive practices which you have noted?

5. In light of our dependence on God and on the land (for examples refer back to study two), how would you define the sins of the people called to judgment in Isaiah 5:11-12?

6. What judgments are given out to those who "have no regard for the deeds of the Lord" (see vv. 13-15)?

Can you identify modern parallels to these judgments?

7. According to verse 15, what crucial attitude shift is necessary for those who have sinned?

8. Compare verses 7 and 16. What is the Lord's motivation in calling his people to account for their abuses of the land and of each other?

Read Hosea 4:1-3.
9. Against whom does the Lord bring a complaint (v. 1)?

10. What are the reasons for the land's mourning (vv. 1-2)?

11. In what ways is our failure to care for the land a failure to acknowledge God?

12. According to this passage, what is the relationship between humans' treatment of one another and their harmony (or lack of it) with the land?

13. *Response:* During the next week, choose a day to fast. For 24 hours, eat no solid foods and drink only water and fruit juice. Set aside time to pray. Meditate on your broken relationship with creation and ask God to lead you to repentance and a new faithfulness.

For Further Study: Compare Genesis 3:17-19 with 1:28-30.

Study 5

A Great Reconciliation

Sin *opened tragic breaches between humans and God, between person* and person, and between humanity and nature. All around us we see the effects of this brokenness.

Jesus died to mend the breach. He died to build a bridge between a loving God and our wounded selves. In relationship to him we are being healed and made new.

This is a great truth. But God never intended for us to stop there—and too often we have. We have forgotten that the gospel means reconciliation between human beings across racial, national, cultural and class boundaries. And we certainly have rarely considered what meaning Jesus' death might have for the created world and our relationship with it.

Read Colossians 1:9-14.

1. What is Paul's prayer for the Colossians (vv. 9-13)?

2. Why do you think Paul prays in this way?

3. How does Paul describe the salvation we have received (vv. 13-14)?

Read Colossians 1:15-23.

4. In verses 15-18, the phrase "he is" recurs three times. What are the titles Paul ascribes to Jesus?

5. What is Jesus' role and activity in relation to nature?

6. What is the scope of Jesus' reconciling work, according to verses 19-20 and verse 23?

7. By what means are all things being reconciled (vv. 20, 22)?

8. List the benefits that Paul says have been given to us through Jesus' death on the cross, according to verses 20-22 and Colossians 2:13-15.

9. What is promised as the result of Jesus' reconciling work in our lives?

10. According to verse 13, "He has rescued us from the dominion of darkness and brought us into the kingdom of the Son." Given the scope of the Son's kingdom described in this passage, how has your understanding of your part in the kingdom and your responsibilities changed?

How can you be a servant of the gospel (v. 23) as it extends to the created world?

11. Return to verses 9-10. Has your knowledge of God's will been expanded through your study of your relationship to his creation?

12. Alone or in your group, read verses 9-14 aloud as your prayer for yourself. Thank God that Jesus has mended your broken relationship with nature, and ask him for love and wisdom to live out that reconciliation.

13. *Response:* Choose one or more of the following activities.

☐ Saving and restoring, two gospel words, have very practical implications for our use of the earth's resources. Begin saving and recycling aluminum cans and newspapers. Donate the pennies you earn to an environmental organization or to an incarnational ministry among the poor.

☐ Solicitation letters and other junk mailings are often printed on only one side of a sheet of paper. Why not save these sheets and write drafts of your school papers on the backs? (The draft of this guide was jotted down on such paper.) Find out, too, whether in your community there is a venue for recycling white bond paper after it has been fully used.

☐ Water—so ordinary, so taken for granted—is a wonderful gift from God. Examine your water-use habits. Perhaps you can take shorter showers. Dishwashers use much more water and electricity than does hand-washing of dishes. A commercial car wash is likewise much more extravagant than bucket-and-rag-style washing in the driveway. How can you save water?

☐ Often people from the Third World can help us see what is wasteful about our lifestyle and how we might live more frugally. Talk to an international student about these issues. He or she may well have some wisdom to offer.

For Further Study: Colossians 1:3-8.

Study 6

Under the Bright Wings

The world is charged with the grandeur of God.
   It will flame out, like shining from shook foil;
   It gathers to a greatness, like the ooze of oil
Crushed. Why do men then now not reck his rod?
Generations have trod, have trod, have trod;
   And all is seared with trade; bleared, smeared with toil;
   And wears man's smudge and shares man's smell: the soil
Is bare now, nor can foot feel, being shod.

And for all this, nature is never spent;
   There lives the dearest freshness deep down things;
And though the last lights off the black West went
   Oh, morning, at the brown brink eastward, springs—
Because the Holy Ghost over the bent
   World broods with warm breast and with ah! bright wings.
           —"God's Grandeur" by Gerard Manley Hopkins

Read Romans 8:18-27.

1. What contrast does Paul make in verse 18?

2. We often speak of being in the "already and not-yet" of the kingdom of God. According to verses 19-21, who/what else has joined us in waiting for the full revelation of the kingdom?

3. How does the contrast in verse 21 shed light on the contrast in verse 18?

4. Based on previous studies (for example, Ps 104), what do you think "bondage to decay" means?

5. Who and what participate in the groans that are described as expressing a longing for full redemption (v. 22)?

6. What are the "firstfruits of the Spirit" that we possess?

7. Read Romans 8:14-17. In what ways has God singled out human beings as special recipients of his grace?

8. Read Genesis 3:17-19. How was creation "subjected to frustration" (Rom 8:20)?

9. In verse 23, how does Paul further explain what he means by glory (v. 18) and glorious freedom (v. 21)?

10. How does Paul define the word *hope* (v. 24)?

In a biblical context do you believe the words *hope* and *waiting* suggest a passive or an active state? Why?

11. How do verses 26-27 describe the Spirit's role in our prayerful waiting for the kingdom's fullness?

12. Bring together the images of the Spirit's work in Genesis 1:2, Romans 8:26-27 and Hopkins's poem (above). How do these pictures enrich your concept of the Spirit's relationship to creation?

13. *Response:* With your small group or other Christian friends, plan an Earthkeeping Day for your fellowship, campus, church or community. Share what God has been unfolding to you about our responsibilities toward the earth, and offer resources to help others begin to practice an earthkeeping ethic.

For Further Study: Romans 8:28-39; Revelation 22:1-5.

Suggestions for Leaders

Leading a Bible discussion can be an enjoyable and rewarding experience. But it can also be intimidating—especially if you've never done it before. If this is how you feel, you're in good company. When God asked Moses to lead the Israelites out of Egypt, he replied, "O Lord, please send someone else to do it!" (Ex 4:13). But God's response to all of his servants—including you—is essentially the same: "My grace is sufficient for you" (2 Cor 12:9).

There is another reason you should feel encouraged. Leading a Bible discussion is not difficult if you follow certain guidelines. You don't need to be an expert on the Bible or a trained teacher. The suggestions listed below should enable you to effectively and enjoyably fulfill your role as leader.

Preparing for the Study

1. Ask God to help you understand and apply the passage in your own life. Unless this happens, you will not be prepared to lead others. Pray too for the various members of the group. Ask God to open your hearts to the message of his Word and motivate you to action.

2. Read the introduction to the entire guide to get an overview of the subject at hand and the issues which will be explored. If you want to do more reading on the topic, check out the resource section at the end of the guide for appropriate books and magazines.

3. As you begin each study, read and reread the assigned Bible passages to familiarize yourself with them. Read the passages suggested for further study as well. This will give you a broader picture of how these issues are discussed throughout Scripture.

4. This study guide is based on the New International Version of the Bible. It will help you and the group if you use this translation as the basis for your study and discussion.

5. Carefully work through each question in the study. Spend time in meditation and reflection as you consider how to respond.

6. Write your thoughts and responses in the space provided in the study guide. This will help you to express your understanding of the passage clearly.

7. It might help you to have a Bible dictionary handy. Use it to look up any unfamiliar words, names or places. (For additional help on how to study a passage, see chapter five of *Leading Bible Discussions,* IVP.)

8. Take the response portion of each study seriously. Consider what this means for your life—what changes you might need to make in your lifestyle and/or actions you need to take in the world. Remember that the group will follow your lead in responding to the studies.

Leading the Study
1. Begin the study on time. Open with prayer, asking God to help the group to understand and apply the passage.

2. Be sure that everyone in your group has a study guide. Encourage the group to prepare beforehand for each discussion by reading the introduction to the guide and by working through the questions in the study.

3. At the beginning of your first time together, explain that these studies are meant to be discussions, not lectures. Encourage the members of the group to participate. However, do not put pressure on those who may be hesitant to speak during the first few sessions.

4. Have a group member read the introductory paragraph at the beginning of the discussion. This will orient the group to the topic of the study.

5. Have a group member read aloud the passage to be studied. (When there is more than one passage, the Scripture is divided up throughout the study so that you won't have to keep several passages in mind at the same time.)

6. As you ask the questions, keep in mind that they are designed to be used just as they are written. You may simply read them aloud. Or you may prefer to express them in your own words. There may be times when it is appropriate to deviate from the study guide. For example, a question may already have been answered. If so, move on to the next question. Or someone may raise an important question not covered in the guide. Take time to discuss it, but try to keep the group from going off on tangents.

7. Avoid answering your own questions. If necessary, repeat or rephrase them until they are clearly understood. An eager group quickly becomes passive and silent if they think the leader will do most of the talking.

8. Don't be afraid of silence. People may need time to think about the question before formulating their answers.

9. Don't be content with just one answer. Ask, "What do the rest of you think?" or "Anything else?" until several people have given answers to the question.

10. Acknowledge all contributions. Try to be affirming whenever possible. Never reject an answer. If it is clearly off-base, ask, "Which verse led you to that conclusion?" or again, "What do the rest of you think?"

11. Don't expect every answer to be addressed to you, even though this will probably happen at first. As group members become more at ease, they will begin to truly interact with each other. This is one sign of healthy discussion.

12. Don't be afraid of controversy. It can be very stimulating. If you don't resolve an issue completely, don't be frustrated. Move on and keep it in mind for later. A subsequent study may solve the problem.

13. Periodically summarize what the group has said about the passage. This helps to draw together the various ideas mentioned and gives continuity to the study. But don't preach.

14. Don't skip over the response question. Be willing to get things started by describing how you have been convicted by the study and what action you'd like to take. Consider doing a service project as a group in response to what you're learning from the studies. Alternately, hold one another accountable to get involved in some kind of active service.

15. Conclude your time together with conversational prayer. Ask for God's help in following through on the commitments you've made.

16. End on time.

Many more suggestions and helps are found in *The Small Group Leader's Handbook* and *Good Things Come in Small Groups* (both from IVP). Reading through one of these books would be worth your time.

Resources

Organizations

Au Sable Institute, 7526 Sunset Trail NE, Mancelona, Minn. 49659; (616) 587-8686. Serves eighty North American colleges with a certified environmental studies program based on biblical principles. The program includes field trips, an annual forum and teaching from scholars and practitioners.

Co-op America, 2100 M St. NW, Suite 310, Washington, D.C. 20063; (202) 872-5307 or (800) 424-2667. An affiliation of organizations and individuals concerned to spend and invest money in products and corporations that promote justice and care for the environment. Publications, travel service, health insurance, financial planning and more.

Eco-Justice Working Group, 475 Riverside Dr., New York, N.Y. 10115; (212) 870-2511. A Christian group that lobbies for legislation to protect the environment and produces resources for churches.

Eleventh Commandment Fellowship, Box 14667, San Francisco, Calif. 94114. A Christian ecology group that—through study groups, educational materials and networking—calls local churches to fight environmental degradation.

Floresta USA, 9230 Trade Place, Suite 100, San Diego, Calif. 92126; (619) 566-6068. A Christian ministry of reforestation and responsible agriculture in the Dominican Republic and, eventually, other developing countries.

Greenpeace, 1436 U St. NW, Washington, D.C. 20009; (202) 462-1177. With offices in several major U.S., Canadian and Australian cities, Greenpeace uses protest and nonviolent direct action to work on behalf of the environment. Membership includes a subscription to the organization's informative bimonthly magazine.

Jubilee/Christian Farmers Federation, 115 Woolwich St., Guelph, Ont. N1H 3V1, Canada; (519) 837-1620. Provides resources and analysis of public policy bearing on stewardship of land. Primarily for farmers.

National Wildlife Federation, 1400 16th St. NW, Washington, D.C. 20036; (202) 797-6800. Goals are to promote conservation of wilderness and wildlife habitat, clean air and water, and other environmental concerns. Publishes several magazines and other educational materials, and lobbies Congress.

Sierra Club, 730 Polk St., San Francisco, Calif. 94109; (415) 776-2211. A lobbying and educational organization concerned particularly with the conservation of wilderness.

Union of Concerned Scientists, 26 Church St., Cambridge, Mass. 02238; (617) 547-5552. An organization of scientists promoting environmental responsibility and offering helpful educational materials.

Publications

Berry, Wendell. *The Unsettling of America: Culture and Agriculture.* San Francisco: Sierra Club Books, 1977. Berry is a respected writer and spokesperson for ecologically sound agriculture. This classic work takes a sweeping look at modern postindustrial culture and then focuses on issues surrounding farming.

Brown, Lester R., et al. *State of the World.* New York: W. W. Norton. A Worldwatch Institute yearbook examining "the world's ecological health."

The Creator's Mandate, 150-207 Castlegreen Dr., Thunder Bay, Ont. P7A 7L8, Canada; (807) 767-9237. A bimonthly newsletter, launched January 1990, for evangelicals wishing to explore issues of the environment.

Faricy, Robert. *Wind and Sea Obey Him: Approaches to a Theology of Nature.* Westminster, Md.: Christian Classics, 1988. A profoundly biblical examination of the relationships among God, human beings and nature.

Garbage: The Practical Journal for the Environment, P.O. Box 51647, Boulder, Colo. 80321-1647; (800) 274-9909. An entertaining, informative bimonthly magazine devoted to practical ways of cutting back on waste and protecting the environment.

Granberg-Michaelson, Wes. *Ecology and Life: Accepting Our Environmental Responsibility.* Waco, Tex.: Word, 1988. Granberg-Michaelson is one of the premier evangelical thinkers in this realm. An important book.

Granberg-Michaelson, Wes, ed. *Tending the Garden: Essays on the Gospel and the Earth.* Grand Rapids: Eerdmans, 1987. A fine collection of thought-provoking essays.

Moltman, Jürgen. *God in Creation: A New Theology of Creation and the Spirit of God.* San Francisco: Harper & Row, 1985. Explores God the Spirit's activity in nature, with special emphasis on his immanence (indwelling presence).

Toxics and Minority Communities. Report available from the Center for Third World Organizing, 3861 Martin Luther King Jr. Way, Oakland, Calif. 94609; (415) 654-9601. Examines U.S. environmental policies and the dumping of toxic wastes in low-income minority communities in the U.S. and in the Third World.

Wilkinson, Loren, ed. *Earthkeeping: Christian Stewardship of Natural Resources.* Grand Rapids: Eerdmans, 1980. A collection of essays that has been hailed as a landmark work.